STOP STROLLING AROUND NAKED IN YOUR BUSINESS EMPIRE LIKE "ALITTLE KINGLY"

"ALITTLE KINGLY"
™ © COPYRIGHT 2009

Put on your business turnaround threads
in the next 24 HOURS!

Write your own A-Z Economic Stimulus Plan
Improve quality
Ramp sales
Reduce expenses
Take advantage of a battered economy
Jump start your business
Supercharge yourself and your employees
Turn your business around
and
Stop being "Alittle Kingly"

Richard W. Linford

Stop Strolling Around Naked in Your Business Empire Like "Alittle Kingly"
© Copyright 2007, 2008, 2009 -- 3rd Edition

"No advice provided herein is legal advice or mandatory business advice. No advice provided herein is financial or investment or securities related advice. The reader is responsible to obtain his or her own legal or business or financial or investment or securities related advice."

Note from the author

I am a businessman, and an attorney at law with an unbundled law practice and experience in business transactions and turnarounds, venture and debt capital, mergers and acquisitions, conventional and pre-construction real estate, intellectual property, licensing, sales and marketing, broadcasting, radio and television brokerage transactions, and art monument sales transactions. I have served as a manager, director, vice president, and COO and CEO for several companies my own included, as multi-county chairman of the Red Cross, as a Junior Achievement and American Heart Association Board member, as state chairman of The National Conference of Christians and Jews and as a national board member. I am active in my Christian faith as a member of The Church of Jesus Christ of Latter-day Saints (Mormon). My blog is http://ceostrategies.blogspot.com/

To your great health, wealth, and happiness.

Best regards,
Richard Linford

Introduction. You know the story of the King who wore no clothes in the parade. In his foolishness and pride he let a couple of con artists sell him a set of non-existent clothes. A little boy standing along the parade route shouted out "The King has no clothes on." Whereupon, the King acknowledged his folly, got dressed, and got rid of the con-men. This little book contains a set of short paragraphs that attempt to shout out "The King has no clothes on" so if you are the king of some domain wake up and do something about it immediately. These concepts are written to trigger your thoughts and your action to improve your business and your life. These are brutal economic times for most if not all. Notwithstanding, you can pull off a business turnaround in this or any economy, while protecting yourself from creditors, predators and competitors, and begin to do so in the next 24 HOURS, by writing your own A to Z Economic Stimulus Plan and by starting to take steps needed to

- Ensure quality
- Accelerate production
- Improve customer service
- Ramp sales
- Reduce expenses
- Take advantage of a battered economy
- Jump start your business
- Supercharge yourself and your employees and
- Turn your business around

This little book is written to help us all stop being "Alittle Kingly."

"No advice provided herein is legal advice or mandatory business advice. No advice provided herein is financial or investment or securities related advice. The reader is responsible to obtain his or her own legal or business or financial or investment or securities related advice."

Contents.

Following are questions and concepts that should help you write your personal and business economic stimulus plan and begin to turn your business around in the next 24 HOURS. Make your notes page by page and use the worksheets or create your own spreadsheets.

Accounting. Do your accountants give you incorrect, general, monthly expense and sales reports? [If they do, insist on correct, specific, weekly accounting reports.]

Advertising and public relations. Are you currently spending a bundle on television, radio, print and public relations with no clue as to whether your expenditure is effectively driving business your way? [If so, think about stopping your advertising for a few months to determine what is happening and at the same time save the money you would have spent on advertising.]

Advertising and public relations. Do you already have an advertising or public relations campaign that appears to be working? [If so, put an immediate moratorium on changing your advertising and public relations copy. Each time you change your advertising or public relations copy you spend more money with your ad agency and media channels and you lose your penetration in the marketplace. Unless you have no advertising or public relations whatsoever, or unless your advertising and public relations are not at all effective, even though you are tired of your advertising or public relations campaign, you may want to stay the course, make no changes, and take a calculated risk that repetition will cause you to run right past your competition. Why? Because you can count on it that each of your competitors will experience a "fresh burst of discontent" with their advertising and public relations campaigns and they will change their advertising and public relations initiatives and in the process they will destroy their penetration in the market place. A little book called **Reality Advertising** by Rosser Reeves is a classic and a good short read.]

Notes:

To buy a hard copy of one of my books, click on **www.amazon.com** and type in the title or my name.

"Alittle Kingly" © **2009. All rights reserved.** You know the story of the King who wore no clothes. In his foolishness and pride he let several con artists sell him a set of non-existent clothes. A little boy standing along the parade route shouted out "The King has no clothes on." Whereupon, the King realized and acknowledged his folly. put on his real threads, and got rid of the con men. This little book contains a set of short paragraphs that attempt to shout out "The King has no clothes on so wake up and get dressed." These concepts are written to trigger our thoughts and our immediate action to improve our business and our life. These are brutal economic times for most if not all. Notwithstanding, we can pull off a business turnaround in this or any economy, while protecting ourselves from creditors, predators and competitors, and we can begin to do so in the next 24 HOURS, by writing our own A to Z Economic Stimulus Plan and by starting to take the steps necessary to --

- Ensure quality
- Accelerate production
- Improve customer service
- Ramp sales
- Reduce expenses
- Take advantage of a battered economy
- Jump start our business
- Supercharge ourself and our employees and
- Turn our business around and
- All the while stop being "Alittle Kingly."

Analyze your business.*** Analyze your financial, legal and operational systems to ferret out opportunities and problems. Your analysis should be based on what you already know. It will be enhanced by interviews with your key managers and workers.

1) Is your organization and are your system(s) functioning well?
2) Is there internal consistency?
3) Are policies in place and are they understandable and adhered to?
5) Are procedures in place and are they understandable and adhered to?
6) Who has responsibility for each policy and procedure?

7) Does each worker in your organization have and understand and implement a written job description?

8) Are assignments clearly made?

9) Are system flows logical and or redundant?

10) Are personnel, financial resources, equipment, plant and real estate resources fully used?

11) How does each piece fit with the other pieces and the whole?

12) How do activities mesh?

13) How do divisional objectives work together?

14) How to plans compliment each other?

15) Are plans reasonable and achievable given competition and economic trends?

16) Are all of your business activities legal?

17) Is equipment maintained or is some of it inefficient and obsolete?

18) Are managers studying and using the performance and other information they have available?

19) How do company activities and products and services relate in theory and in practice to industry standards and models?

20) Do your organization and its activities fit the standard organization and activity models for the industry you are in?

21) If there are deviations from the norm are they necessary? Are they warranted?

22) Are the methods and procedures you use in line with industry practices and procedures and standards for things like maintenance, quality, purchasing, estimating, and appraising?

23) Is your company performance in line with industry gross margins and return on equity?

24) What if any are the problems?

25) Does your business organization and its parts really work?

26) Are you losing money because you have costly layers of management or workers?

27) Is there confusion about who does what?

28) Is there confusion about stewardships? About authority?

29) Is there inappropriate or inefficient or unproductive matching of authority and responsibilities?

30) What are your financial, legal and organizational weaknesses?

31) How can each weakness best be dealt with and mitigated or eliminated?

Notes:

Annual report. Does your annual report contain inaccurate or misleading information? [You may want to read several of Warren Buffett's annual reports on the internet and use his approach as a template in writing and issuing a decent short annual report.]

Apprentices. Who are your apprentices? [Who is learning the business to take it over when for some reason you can't lead and perform?]

Arbitration, mediation and litigation. Are you in the middle of litigation or arbitration or mediation? [If you are, why not get in your car and go see any antagonist and privately work it out face to face. Why not settle immediately. (90% of cases settle anyway so why not be proactive.) If you can't work it out face to face, get your CFO to mediate. If he or she can't pull off mediation, ask your attorney to serve as independent mediator. If matters are still unresolved, try an arbitrator. As last resort litigate.]

Ask for help. Do you believe you can turn your business around on your own? [If so, more power to you. Truth is you probably can't go it on your own. You may need to ask your employees, co-workers, boss, attorney, CPA, insurance person, ad agency, suppliers, customers, or others you know for their wisdom and help.]

Auditing. Do you criticize and fight your auditors? [Although such is an old bad joke, your auditors are not at your business to bayonet the wounded after the battle is over. Your auditors can be of immense help if you ask them not just for financial audit points but also ask them for feedback about management and financial and operational changes you ought to make.]

Notes:

Audit objectives.*** You can work with your auditors and set your own audit objectives. An audit can help you verify
1) that plans for the business are in writing and are followed;
2) that sound business requirements and practices are adhered to;
3) that financial and legal controls are effective and complied with.
4) that activities are prudent and legal.
A good written audit report can document those steps to be taken to turn your business around.

Said another way, an internal and or operational audit can:
a) assess efficiency and effectiveness of performance;
b) identify problems and opportunities for improvement; and
c) develop recommendations for improvement or further action.

Whereas most audits focus on financial controls and only incidentally on how a business may succeed or fail, in its highest form, an audit can identify and evaluate ways your business can fail as well as ways your business can succeed.

Automobiles. Do you provide cars for your sales force. [Why not get rid of most if not all of your fleet today. There is strong argument that anyone other than a sales person should drive his or her own car. There is strong argument that your sales persons should drive their own cars. Why? Because people care about their own property more than they care about yours.]

Notes:

Bankers (emphasizing commercial loan officers), CPAs, attorneys, ad agency people, real estate agents and brokers, and suppliers. Does any one of the above mentioned persons, or for that matter any other professional you deal with on a consistent basis, fail to return your calls or emails same day, not take your calls personally, put you off, keep you waiting, keep asking you for more and more and more information, demonstrate clear inability to make or obtain prompt decisions that affect your business? Does any one of the above still not know your name, know precious little about your business, not care if you succeed or fail, and clearly fail at rendering decent customer service? Is any one of the above persons caught up in his or her own ego and importance? Has any one of the above at any time given you that nagging thought that he or she secretly wants your business to fail? Does any one of the above make you feel inferior and even like dirt when you are in his or her office or presence or on the phone? Does any one of the above have some if not all of the earmarks of incompetence? [If so, why wait and exacerbate an already painful relationship? Why not part company with that person or set of persons right now.]

Beat Yesterday! Set up a chart that shows yesterday and today side by side. [Then beat yesterday.]

Borrowing. Are you borrowing money regularly to meet your credit card payments or other business obligations? [Borrowing to make credit payments or meet your business obligations is an indication that your business is in serious trouble and may be heading for bankruptcy.]

Budget. Do you operate without a written budget and budget hearings? If you have a written budget, do you track expenditures and sales against your budget? [In a very short time if you put your mind to it, you can develop a written budget and get sign-off and buy in from management and from your board and from those who are responsible to implement the budget.]

Business turnaround. Do you believe it can't be done? [If so, set goals, focus, and write your business turnaround economic stimulus plan in the next 4 HOURS. Begin to implement it in the next 20 HOURS. You can if you will. You will if you will.]

Cash. Are there ways in which you are losing or wasting or squandering your cash? [Increase your cash reserves. Collect your cash. Build your cash flow. Husband your cash. Obtain an infusion of non-debt cash. Sell assets that don't produce cash and turn them into cash. Focus on and finish projects that generate cash. Promptly invoice and collect your cash receivables. Inventory all of your personnel and physical assets that have potential and actual "cash value."]

Notes:

To buy a hard copy of one of my books, click www.amazon.com and click on books and type in the title or my name.

CEO and CFO and CIO and COO as best salesmen. Do you believe that only the appointed and anointed sales force can sell your products or services? [What would you think if I told you that the CEO, CFO, CIO, and COO are probably the best salesmen for the company? If you are the CEO or CFO or CIO or COO, you are probably the best sales person in the company simply because you know the business and you know the product and the service. Why not take several minutes right now and make a list of prospects. Pick up the phone and make an appointment to sell. Better yet, why not get your backside out of your chair and call on those potential clients right NOW! Cold turkey! "You can't sell beer to a desk!" is a famous saying of the uncle of the CEO of the Boston Beer Company. The corollary is "You can't sell beer to a computer!"]

CEO's chair. Do you spend a majority of your time at the office sitting on your backside in your chair? [Why not give your chair away and manage your company out of your brief case or laptop by walking around? Why not sell your products and services by getting out of your office to meet face to face with your potential customers and your existing customers. Why not cut your costs today by visiting and negotiating better pricing from your suppliers? Why not stop sitting and get out on the floor of your shop and talk to your workers and make a real difference?]

Cheese. Have you read "Who Moved My Cheese?" If not, check the summary out on Wikipedia and buy yourself a copy. [Bottom line: The cheese supply is always a moving target. So get moving and create or find more cheese.]

Collections. When was the last time you personally reviewed your accounts receivable and collected your money? [Nothing happens until something is sold, billed, collected, banked, and properly allocated.]

Communication. Is there any chance that a communications audit would show that a great majority of your communications day to day are with your cronies or of little value? [Make sure you communicate with each level including each person little or big up and down your organization. Also, have a communications auditor from a private company or from your organization call all of your phone numbers and see what response you get. You will be surprised how many of your employees do not answer their phones. And this is especially true of banks.]

Community service. Are you blocking the United Way and other non-profit representatives who come to your office? [Give something to the community and it will come back to you good measure pressed down and running over.(Luke 6:38)]

Compassion and kindness. Is there any chance a survey of your employees will confirm that you are a mean, hard nosed ogre and that you are not well liked. [In all of this turnaround work, as well each day of the week, there needs to be compassion and kindness tempered with wisdom, for the elderly, for the disabled, for those who are honestly trying, for women who more often than not are treated as second class citizens and are bumping against glass ceilings, for anyone who is disadvantaged, in short, for anyone who works with and for you, or for whom you work.]

Compensation. Is your compensation plan tied to results? [If not, it ought to be. Write your own compensation plan designed to motivate and reward your people for their performance. Pay for performance. Perks for performance. Fun and food for performance. Appropriate gifts for performance.]

Computers. Do your employees play solitaire or other games or shop or surf the internet or do porn or run their own businesses on your nickel? Do they do their finances or their other personal work or spend long lunch breaks or bathroom breaks or social breaks on your time on your dime? [If so, inform them in a nice or not so nice way that you own their time and you own the computers they use. They owe you and the company a good eight hour day's work if you are on a five day work week and more if you are on a four day week. Tell them you expect each of them to give the company a solid full day's work in return for a solid full day's pay, perks, fun and food, and appropriate gifts, as well as benefits. It may be more productive in the short and long run and where needed to have this conversation in private one on one rather than in a group setting.]

Confidentiality. Do you boast or inadvertently open your mouth and tell everyone and anyone the names of your customers, your trade secrets, your business plans, the names of your suppliers, how you do things, your finances, your timelines, details about your family, information about your assets? [If so, to be blunt, you may want to "put a rag in it!" This is a common sense personal, family and business safety and security measure. Not even your relatives deserve to know.]

Conflict of interest. Do you let your employees operate their own businesses or carry out their agendas on your time, equipment and dollar? Do your employees take equipment home and work on their own businesses? Do they sell their own products from your telephones, or from your computers on eBay? Do they surf the Internet or gamble from your premises and phones and computer equipment? [Make it clear by policy and lecture that you cannot afford the brain, time, and financial drain. Why should you pay to develop your employee's business or subsidize his or her game of solitaire? To do so doesn't make sense. Part company with those who won't focus in support of your enterprise.]

Consultants. Are you paying consultants and human relations process engineers big bucks? If so, think about firing them all in the next thirty minutes. The definition of 99% of consultants is "a person who comes to your business to listen to your employees and then to listen to you or vice versa and then to write you a report telling you what you or your employees told them." So be your own consultant. Use the forms at the back of this little book or your own and write and implement your own economic stimulus plan.]

Continuing education. When was the last time you sharpened your saw by signing up for continuing education course work?

Contracts and agreements. Are you or any of your management team or workers guilty of making ORAL sales or other contracts and agreements? [Unequivocally, no long lasting specifically enforceable employee or customer relationship will ever be in place properly until there is a written, signed sales or other pertinent agreement. Put a sign up in your business that says: THERE ARE AND WILL BE NO ORAL AGREEMENTS OR CONCESSIONS OR DISCOUNTS OR CONTRACTS! EVERY AGREEMENT OR CONCESSION OR DISCOUNT OR CONTRACT MUST BE IN WRITING, MUST FIRST BE REVIEWED BY MY ATTORNEY AND BY MY BOARD, AND MUST BE SIGNED BY ME!! ANY OTHER CONVERSATION IS SIMPLY DISCUSSION.]

Contracting. Are you guilty of favoritism in your contracting? [If so, keep in mind that it is not what a person says or who a person knows or is related to. It is what a person or business does in your behalf and how well and how timely and how inexpensively they do it.]

14

Corporate restructuring. Can the same people who have been working with you all this time pull off a significant turnaround of your business? [Maybe they can. Maybe they can't. Odds are they can't or they would have done it already. You may need to restructure your company which probably includes gradually or immediately bringing in new talent capable of creating the turnaround and capable of managing the enterprise after turnaround initiatives have been approved and carried out. Notwithstanding, DO NOT HIRE ANYONE UNTIL YOU SIT DOWN AT YOUR DESK AND MATHEMATICALLY CALCULATE HOW MUCH MONEY YOU WILL PAY THEM PER MONTH, PER YEAR, PER TWO YEARS, PER FIVE YEARS, PER TEN YEARS. It is your money. Believe it or not, the fastest way to lose your money and suffer your own private recession or depression may be by making a new hire or new hires!]

Correspondence and talking. Are you guilty of writing and talking too much? [If you can't write your memo on one page front only, there is good argument you don't know what you are talking about. If you are in the habit of pontificating, keep in mind that in business, listening always beats talking hands down. We have two ears so we will listen twice as much as we talk.]

Costs. Are you paying too much for everything? [Are there ways you can negotiate with your suppliers and cut your costs? If your present suppliers are not working out for you, is it time to get new ones? And get second bids. And say to each bidder: "I need your help to keep my costs down so I can stay in business." And say to them after you receive their bid, "Is that the very best you can do?"]

Notes:

Credibility. Do you believe you can do nothing to bolster your credibility in the community? [Your credibility is based on what you do and not on what you say so get out of your chair and do something. Cut costs. Jump start revenues. Restructure. Make it happen now. Help the needy. Give to the United Way. On the flip side, credibility can be enhanced with the help of a good public relations person.]

Customers and Sales Persons. Are you serving a group of customers who don't buy from you and don't pay you? [Can you fire thirty to sixty percent of your customers and not lose a penny in revenues or relationships in the process? And is the same true of your sales force? Are twenty percent of your sales persons generating eighty percent of your sales?]

Customer service. Are you ignoring your customers? [You need to take a day and think like your customer. You need to thank and help your customer because you like your customer. You need to meet with your customer personally because your customer is the lifeblood of your company.]

Customers: TEN MOST IMPORTANT. Who are your ten most important customers? Are you ignoring those ten most important customers? [Make a list of those ten. Stop what you are doing. Get in your car or on an airplane and go see those ten customers. Focus your attention first on serving those ten most important customers. Then worry about the rest.]

Credit cards. Is there any way under the sun that you can stop some if not all credit card use in the company in the next few hours? [What would happen if you gathered up all business credit cards and cancelled all of them? Ninety percent of them? If there is any way you can cut off that 20%+ credit card interest, it will be to your advantage. If you are personally living on credit cards and paying steep interest fees the same principle applies.]

Notes:

Credit terms. Do you accept any and all credit terms? [What will happen if you stop accepting all credit terms unless absolutely necessary? What will happen if you establish "high" credit terms immediately? What will happen to revenues and profits if you require 50% down paid immediately and the 50% remaining balance at completion prior to delivery?]

Creditors. Are you having trouble dealing with your creditors? [Do you believe that you cannot deal with your creditors? Can you meet with them immediately? Can you ask your creditors to eliminate finance and interest charges? Ask them to reduce the amount of your loan. Ask them to give you more time. Ask them today to forgive your debt altogether.]

Crisis management. How valuable might it be to stop what you are doing today and write a crisis management plan even though there is or may be no crisis? Would it be prudent to implement the crisis management plan and do periodic training and drills to avert or ameliorate such a crisis. [What will happen to you and your family and the business if there is

1) A flood?
2) A fire?
3) An earthquake?
4) A theft?
5) Employee vandalism?
6) A gang incident?
7) Terrorism?
8) A war?
9) A major long lasting illness of yourself or a key employee or employees?
10) Loss or death of a key employee or employees?
11) A disgruntled employee?
12) A crime?
13) Loss of critical equipment?
14) Loss of financing?
15) A Sexual Harassment lawsuit?

Cut costs. Do you have to continue spending as much as you have spent in the past? [Why not take a few minutes right now and identify and cut all unnecessary expenses? Cut costs everywhere? Cut costs creatively? Cut unnecessary lunches? Ask others to pay their share of the bill? Start thinking that every dollar belongs to your wife or husband and you have to account to her or him tonight for that dollar! Tighten your grip and put a lock on your money clip.]

Damaging activities. Is there anything you are doing personally that is damaging to your business and that does or can hurt you or your family or business badly? [Make a list of anything and everything that you know hurts you or your family or your business. Take necessary actions to counteract anything which hurts or is hurting you. For example: spending or misusing company resources, sexual harassment, violation of law, etc.]

Danger signs. What are the critical danger signs that your business is sick? Are you ignoring those danger signs? [List and analyze the danger signs that tell you your business is sick and do something about each item on your list if it is not already too late.]

Debt consolidation. How are you dealing with your debts? [Consolidate your debts and cut your interest costs and arrange lower payments.]

Debt financing. Are you dead set on keeping your business afloat with debt financing? [Is it possible to change your mind set and start getting out of debt today. Pay off your smallest debt today. Then work on the next. Then the next. Interest never sleeps. As you pay off one debt, apply the money you save to pay off other debts until you are debt free.]

Debt restructuring. Do you have to keep living with your current debt structure? [How about cramming down each creditor 30-50-60% today. Where at all possible and prudent, visit with each creditor and say nicely (don't ask): "We are in trouble. Our revenues are off. Our expenses are too high. I have to cut expenses. I have to jump start sales. I can only pay you 50% on the dollar."]

Debt-to-asset ratios. What is your debt to asset ratio? [Your DTA is an indicator your business is in trouble any time you see a rising debt-to-asset ratio.]

Deferred maintenance. How much deferred maintenance are you carrying on your books? For your physical plant? For your cars and equipment? Identify and document all deferred maintenance. [Budget and build a fund to cover present and future maintenance including roof repair, equipment maintenance, concrete and road base repair. If you don't already have one, write and follow a separate budget for maintenance.]

Discussion. Discuss major issues and especially turnaround issues with your management and workers? [By doing so, you demonstrate your approval of recommended turnaround activities. You can put in place a way to track progress. You gain management and worker consensus. A turnaround becomes a cooperative effort.]

Domain names, trademarks and copyrights and licensing and other contracts. Are all of your domain names and trademarks and copyrights and licensing and other contracts inventoried and protected? [As an aside, keep in mind that GoDaddy will only tap your credit card for your domains if your credit card on file is current and valid.]

Downsizing. How important is it that you keep your current headcount? [You can downsize and cut serious expense if you want to badly enough. Would such an initiative improve your productivity and bottom line? In all downsizing, your first thought ought to be to look after those employees who have given their all to your business. Who are they? What have they done for you? How can you downsize yet still maintain your business productivity and help critical faithful employees maintain and increase their standard of living?]

Notes:

Drug free and alcohol free and tobacco free workplace. Are you or any of your employees using illicit drugs? Abusing over the counter drugs? [Stop employing anyone using alcohol or tobacco or marijuana or meth or Oxycontin or any other illicit drug on the job or at the job site. Maintain an alcohol and tobacco and drug free work place. Require mandatory drug testing of all employees including management. Stamp out all alcohol or tobacco or drug use on the job or at the job site. The greatest risk of loss to your company walks in on two legs each day and this is absolutely true of those who use alcohol or tobacco or drugs on the job. And the same is true of those who abuse over the counter drugs. And while you are if there are smoking venues at your company, eliminate any passive cigarette or cigar smoke.]

Email and text messaging and cell phone use. Have you mastered email and text messaging and do you use them? [Email and text messaging can be most powerful personal and business communications tools. Use them to speed up and document your selling and other communication processes and save time. It should be policy that employees not text or talk on a cell phone while driving. Personal email and text messaging and cell phone use on the job should be minimal.]

Emergency preparedness. Do you believe it can't or won't ever happen to you? [Truth is, it can! Accident, Flood. Fire. Terrorist attack. Hurricane. Tornado. Ice storm. Crime. Snow storm. Rain storm. Sickness. Accident. Loss of business. Loss of sales. Loss of critical customers or suppliers. Loss of key commodities. Loss of key or other employees. Loss of a particular customer job. Food shortage. Water contamination. Heat wave. Cold spell. Economic and business downturn. Stock market losses. Theft. So prepare now. And buy needed insurance where prudent. Prepare in advance. If you are prepared you won't fear. At least you won't fear as much.]

Empowerment of your employees. Are you so paranoid and controlling that you keep all control and authority and power personally or at the top of your organization? [Empower your people at every level to "stop or start your assembly line." Empower your people at every level to get things done.]

Notes:

Entry activities for your internal or operational audit.*** If you are engaging internal auditors to conduct a financial and operational audit, a right tone for such an engagement is set at the beginning. Cooperation is critical because if done well the audit can help you produce the end result of turning around and improving your business and its systems. Your operating personnel will have to implement any of the audit findings you approve and if you are conducting your own internal and operational audit and analysis, the same is true. You will need initial understanding and consensus/buy in from your staff and from your managers and operating personnel again because they will have to implement your findings. Up-front, everyone needs to know and agree that all programs and activities and controls are fair game and will be looked at and analyzed critically to ensure that their contribution to the enterprise is warranted and satisfactory. If you employ an outside person or firm to conduct your internal or operational audit, your objective should be to achieve an outside in look with on-going opportunity to discuss and present and test different views of the enterprise. Any outside or internal auditor must have your ear and the ear of the highest authorities in your business organization in order to help you gain the greatest value from the audit. Outside or internal auditors will be able to take time to look systematically at problems and opportunities of your business. Possibly your outside or internal auditors will have skills you don't have within your organization. In all this, keep in mind that a tongue in cheek but often true definition of an auditor is one who comes in after the battle is over to bayonet the wounded. Another definition is that the auditor as with a consultant asks you what is wrong with your business and then writes a lengthy very expensive report to tell you what you told them. That type of audit activity is not without its value but if you know what is wrong and you can document it in writing and fix it, you are smart to do so and you will save yourself a serious bundle of cash you would have paid out to the auditors or consultants.

Notes:

To buy a hard copy of one of my books, click on www.amazon.com and click on books and type in the title or my name.

Equipment and tools. Are you wasting your equipment and tools? [Maintain them. Repair them. Fix them up. Inventory them. Use them to generate wealth and to prosper. Know where your equipment and tools are. Has any employee taken and kept your equipment or tools? If so, you know what to do about it.]

Ethics and Illegality. Do you know of any unethical or illegal conduct, policies, procedures, and or activities in your business? [You and your employees need to be scrupulously ethical and legal in all you do. No unethical or illegal practice or activity goes long without punishment.]

Evaluation. Do you systematically evaluate your progress? [Evaluation is systematic gathering of information about the different facets of your business in order to determine their value and success and failure as compared to a set of criteria or standards. One formula is a cycle: write goals with budget and pro forma and standards, take action, evaluate success or failure compared to standards, reset goals and adjust budget and pro forma and standards, take action, evaluate success or failure, reset goals.]

Excellence. Is there a way in the next five minutes as a matter of policy you can stop accepting all shoddy performance and production? [By expecting excellence and by empowering workers and others to provide quality performance and production, your workers and others will give you the quality and excellence you want and deserve.]

Exit strategies. What is your exit strategy and timing? [You may have choices. Buy. Sell. Merge. Acquire. License. Issue stock. Do a reverse merger. Go public. Give all or some of it away to a 501 C3 and take a tax break.]

Notes:

Failure avoidance. Is there a meaningful way right now you can stop focusing so much on the idea of SUCCESS? [Instead focus on and eliminate what makes you fail? Focus on failure avoidance. Success is a by product of locking in place principles and practices that generate revenues and profits, cut and minimize expenses, and avoid failure.]

Financials. When would you like to stop accepting shoddy or incomplete financials? [Demand solid timely financials from your accountants. Review them regularly. Require cash forecasts and statements monthly, weekly and daily.]

Financing. Are you spending a Lion's share of your time trying to find financing when you need it. [Find and put in place financing before you need it.]

Financing and the CEO. If you are the CEO, it may be smart to stop wasting your time hunting for financing. [Instead, from now on focus all of your energy on increasing high quality repeat sales. Let your CFO look for financing. At least focus three quarters of your time on sales.]

Firing. Have you fired the wrong people? [As you conduct your own management audit and analysis, take a hard look at what people have done and do, not what they say they did and do! Identify what each person is actually doing not what he or she says he or she is doing. Tell your employees what you expect. After a short turnaround grace period, give some thought to firing the worst of those who are not doing what you asked them to do. The Donald Trump "You're fired!" works when you have the facts. The flip side is to take time and keep and find the right people and say: "You're still hired!" or "You're hired." And before you let a subordinate fire or hire a person, you may want to interview that person and review the economic and social impact to the company.]

Notes:

Fix it up. Is there a way you can stop buying new equipment? [Can you put a moratorium on buying new equipment for a time? Where new equipment is thought to be needed, figure out if it is cost effective to keep and fix up and depreciate the old equipment.]

Free. Does your mindset suggest you have to pay for the lunch or whatever? [Ask the other guy to cover the bill. Let suppliers or buyers or customers cover the bill. Check to see if what you need is available free on the internet or from a supplier or from a competitor or customer? Make a list of what you need. Check to see if it is free.]

Freeloaders. Are there freeloaders on your payroll? [One of your smartest decisions may be to identify the freeloaders and help outplace them to another company.]

Gambling. Are any of your workers gambling on your time or for that matter on their own time? [If you have gambling employees on your payroll, it may be timely to stamp out worker gambling at your business. [People gamble in Las Vegas and Atlantic City and on the reservations. Your business is not Las Vegas or Atlantic City or a reservation and should be governed and driven by high principles and should not be a haven for employees who gamble.]

Notes:

Give. Do you know about the Law of Giving? [It is: "Give, and it shall be given unto you; good measure, pressed down, and shaken together, and running over, shall men give into your bosom. For with the same measure that ye mete withal it shall be measured to you again." (Luke 6:38; Isaiah 58.) Give to the poor and needy and God will bless you and your business with the increase you need and want. Give to your customer and he or she will give their business to you. Give your time and love to your aged parents and family and they will love and honor you. I heard a story about a family with an aged father who drooled. It was all family members could do to see him in that condition so the married son and daughter set a separate little table in a far corner of the kitchen and got a large wide wooden bowl from which the aged dad could eat so it would catch his drool and all this would be out of the visual sight of the family and children at the dinner table. One day the married son noticed his little five year old boy in his room whittling on a piece of wood. He asked what he was doing. The little boy said: "Oh, I'm just making a wooden bowl so that when you and mom are old you can sit at the little table in the corner of the kitchen and have something to eat out of so it will catch your drool." The dad and mom were mortified. That evening they set a place at the table for grandpa and figured out a decent way to help him eat.]

Notes:

God's name, swearing, tithing and honoring God. Does anyone at your business, yourself included, take the name of God in vain and swear? Are you familiar with the Law of Tithing? And have you heard the idea that "THE PERSON WHO HONORS GOD IS HONORED BY GOD!" [You may want to give serious thought to putting in place policies and procedures that stop letting anyone in your company take the name of God in vain, policies and procedures that mandate a serious penalty against anyone who does so, yourself included. The Bible Ten Commandments states in Exodus 20:7 "Thou shalt not take the name of the LORD thy God in vain; for the LORD will not hold him guiltless that taketh his name in vain." Anyone in a business, the boss included, who consistently swears using God's name in vain or four letter or other swear words deserves to be reprimanded and if the conduct does not stop to be fired. Just like employees deserve a tobacco smoke free environment in which to work, they also deserve a swearing free environment in which to work. Also, you may want to consider the Bible book of Malachi chapter 3 verses 8 and 9 which say that we as a people have robbed God by not paying tithes and offerings. In verse 10, He challenges us to put Him to the test, pay tithes and offerings and see if He will not open the windows of heaven and shower down blessings upon us. If you do not already do so, you may want to think about the blessings that come from honoring God and from dedicating a tithing ten percent or some percentage of your income to God. If you do, the promise is He will honor and bless you and your business and your family. I have a friend Stan Watts, a now world renowned sculptor, who decided one day he would dedicate his talents and business to God and from that moment God's blessings poured down upon him and his business.]

Graphics. Are your written communications boring? Do your written communications suffer from plainness and lack of creativity? [All the desktop publishing tools you could want are available for reasonable money. You don't have to use shoddy graphics.]

Green. Are you buying and providing "brown" when you can be buying and providing "green?" [There are plenty of products and services and energy sources now that are green.]

Notes:

Gross margins. Is your business suffering and anemic because your gross margins are low? [Why not set in writing minimum gross margins your company can and ought to and will tolerate? Better yet, why not raise and set high margins and write them in a policy and stick to them? You are no doubt worth every penny so ask for and get the $ margins you are worth?]

Headcount reduction. Are you carrying bloated headcount? [See if you can cut your headcount by 50% today.]

Hiring enough people. Do you have the headcount you need? [If you need added headcount run the ads and hire more people.]

Hiring and Firing the wrong people. Have you hired and or fired the wrong people? [Hire people who can and have done it "with excellence" and who can prove they have done so. Don't just hire those who look good and dress well and talk smoothly and say they want to do it or say they have done it. Do your homework. Check them out. Hire those who do and have actually done it. None of this negates the need to provide opportunities for those who will make good apprentices. Same goes for firing. Don't fire the people who can and have done it. You can put up with a few idiosyncrasies.]

Honesty. Can you think of one reason not to be scrupulously honest? Can you think of one reason not to only hire and keep employees who are scrupulously honest?

How can I help you? These may well be the five most powerful words in business and life! A young man named Michael Bradshaw once reported to me. This was not just his motto. He asked the question and he gave what time and energy and talent were needed and helpful. He was considered one if not the most valuable employee in the company.

Humor. Are you dour, grouchy and serious? [Good humor makes your business a fun pleasant place for management, workers, customers, and the public.]

Improvement. How can you stop any losses today? [Set up a chart showing losses yesterday and today. Then "Beat Yesterday and Today."]

Insurance. Are you under the impression that it simply can't happen to you or your business. [Truth is, "It can and it probably will." You aren't exempt. Buy needed insurance coverage today. Buy term life. Buy enough casualty insurance. Have adequate fire insurance. Buy E&O insurance. Get yourself a good honest insurance agent.]

Integrity. Is there any thought you can be dishonest and get away with it in any way or under any circumstance? [Even the smallest amount of dishonesty will out and destroy you.]

Internal and operational audit steps.*** A conventional internal and operational audit includes these steps: ENTRY; SURVEY; ANALYSIS; ISSUE IDENTIFICATION; DISCUSSION; TESTWORK AND RESEARCH; REPORTING; EVALUATION OF FINDINGS; APPROVAL OF ACTION STEPS; IMPLEMENTATION; AND EVALUATION OF PROGRESS.

Investing Wisely. Some believe they can invest in stocks or bonds or real estate or collectibles by "feel or gut instinct or by blindly following the recommendation of some stock broker, analyst or guru?" [Truth is you can't. Ben Graham's book "The Intelligent Investor" is the source of much of Warren Buffett's wisdom. It is perhaps the best book on intelligent investing ever written. If you are going to invest you need a written plan stating your investment principles. Then you need a tracking system to help ensure that you follow your plan and adhere to those principles.]

Notes:

IRS. Are you or anyone in your business cheating the IRS? [File on time. File truthfully. Pay truthfully. Cut taxes where lawful. At all cost, pay your payroll and FICA taxes. It is a federal crime to fail to file and pay your taxes and failure to file and pay is punishable by stiff fines and jail time in federal penitentiaries not to mention civil penalties.]

Issues. Do you understand all of the issues that impact your business? [Write and maintain a written list of all possible issues that affect your business.]

Issue identification as part of your internal or operational audit.*** From analysis of your business should flow a set of issues to be reviewed by you and your management and worker teams. Issues are questionable matters and possible recommendations and audit findings. Issues ought to be stated in a standard format that includes the traditional elements of an audit finding including:
1) Statement of the problem or opportunity or condition or need or difficulty that requires attention;
2) cause of such;
3) significance of such;
4) criteria and standards;
5) recommendation to fix or adjust or solve or take advantage of an opportunity together with added advise as to how to do so.

Issues ought to be listed in order of priority.

Priority issues include problems arising from illegal or unethical conduct and any confusion of objectives or stewardship or policy because such jeopardize the overall business and its owners and management and cause management and other workers to be less effective. Top of any such list is management or worker competence or fit for particular jobs or assignments. Some people are not competent for the task assigned. Lack of financial and legal controls or violation, computer and technology and software needs, information blockages hinder progress of the whole organization.

Late past due payments. Are you paying your suppliers or your employees or others late? [Always pay all obligations precisely on time when you have the money to pay. Late payments telegraph the message that your business is sick. Late payments reinforce that fact to all who work for you and all who do business with you. Late payments depress morale and trigger negative feelings of workers, suppliers, professional persons, and creditors. And this is especially true when it comes to making payroll on time.]

Law and a good attorney. Are you or anyone in your business or is the business itself breaking the law? [There is no mercy in the IRS or the criminal justice system or in business. Justice will be satisfied. If the law is broken someone will pay the consequences either in dollars or often in jail time. Ask your attorney to review your practices and tell you if he thinks you are breaking the law in any way.]

Layoffs. Is your business hemorrhaging? [If so, stop the bleeding now including making any needed reduction in pay or reduction in force.]

Notes:

Leadership. Are you and those in your business blindly following others in or out of your industry? [Are there ways you can lead out and innovate? Are there ways you can lead out and sell? Leaders don't pontificate and make excuses. Leaders get even and get ahead by selling better than the competition.]

Leasing. Would leasing instead of buying equipment, cars, and real estate make sense? [Leasing requires careful analysis.]

Legal Matters. Are any legal matters dragging on? [Take the initiative and calculate the cost either way and if it is wise settle today and get on with your life and focus your energy on sales. Otherwise, get a good litigator and litigate the matter with serious energy and force. More than 90% of legal matters settle so why not go to anyone threatening or instituting legal action and settle the matter now.]

Notes:

To buy a hard copy of one of my books, click on www.amazon.com and click on books and type in the title or my name.

Litigation. Are you conducting any half hearted litigation? [If you decide for whatever reason that you must litigate, and if it is apparent to you that your adversary will not accept your olive branch and settle, then put your finest litigator gladiators in the arena, engage with full force, slay the lions and the tigers, slay the opposing gladiators, beat your opponent and settle big time or win your case outright and get a judgment and collect what is due and owing.]

Losses. If your company is hemorrhaging in any way, during the next 120 minutes tie on the tourniquet. [Have your CFO bring you a memo in the next 60 minutes showing you how you can cut your costs immediately and increase your revenues by half or more. Then if possible right now implement the good ideas she or he brings you.]

Notes:

Lottery. Is there any hint that your business is being operated by chance or like the lottery? [Business is not a chance activity. Business is the act of taking a quality product or service to market such that a buyer will pay for it with hard currency.]

Maintenance deferred. Can you think of any deferred maintenance in your business? [Deferred maintenance of buildings, infrastructure, equipment, automobiles and trucks, computers and software, and any other systems, is slow cancer death to your business. See **Deferred maintenance**.]

Management principles. Is your business operating on sound management principles? [A great business is governed by right business principles. It is management's job to identify those right principles, follow them, bring in the revenues, pay the bills, cut the expenses, and establish long term profitability.]

Notes:

Managers. Are your managers expected to be leaders or visionaries? [Normally, such is a waste of their time and yours because by definition it isn't possible for a manager to lead and be visionary. Leaders lead and are visionary. Managers manage and follow the direction of the leader. It is your job to lead and be the visionary for the company.]

Marketing. Is there indication that your marketing is a random hit and miss process? [Do you have in place a written marketing, advertising and public relations plan that makes you stretch and that focuses on selling to target groups of specific buyers. Look at guerilla marketing and advertising and public relations methods including viral email systems and website traffic builders and social networking.]

Marriage and family. How distant are you from your spouse? [Your marriage and family are the most important parts of your life so give serious thought to spending more quality time with your spouse and children and grandchildren. The business will always be there until you exit. The special anniversary or birthday or little league game - each happens only once.]

Notes:

Mediation. [See Arbitration, mediation and litigation above.]

Morale. Is it possible you are personally responsible for causing any negative morale in your organization? [Bad morale destroys your business. Explain to your people the need for a turnaround. Explain to your people your turnaround plans. Get their buy-in and participation. Tell them you are not asking for their consent. Tell them how important the functions and work are that they perform. An employee's morale is a simple function and result of knowing that those functions and the specific work that he or she performs are important and vital to the enterprise and that he or she is being paid a reasonable amount and on time for his or her labor. Show your people how important their functions and their work are to the success of the business and pay them on time with periodic raises and bonuses and their morale will be high and they will help you make your business a success.]

Motivation. Some including the "Recognition Companies" argue that motivation is not a function of money. [Truth is it is a huge myth that motivation in business is a function of food and games and company Christmas and summer parties and gold watches and other such gifts and recognition plaques and certificates and golf outings and similar perks. Motivation of the employee in this century economy and business is strictly a function of money and money related benefits paid to the employee for a particular set of actions.]

Multi-media. Are you using complex multi-media when simple one dimensional media will do the job? [Complexity is the enemy of communication in the sales presentation, board room, management or sales meeting, and on the internet. If a one page front only memo will do the job, use it. There is a good argument that power point presentations are bogus and tend to obfuscate rather than enlighten.]

Notes:

Naked business men and sharks. Harvey McKay's books teach us to identify and stop dealing with people who have no money and no experience and no skill and no connections and to stop dealing with cut throat con-men sharks. [Read Harvey McKay's "Beware the Naked Man Who Offers You His Shirt."]

Negativity. On a scale of one to ten how negative are your thoughts? [You may want to study and implement in your life the law of attraction which says that you receive positive results if you think positive thoughts. It seems to be a law of the universe that you get what you think about -- usually no less and usually no more.]

Negotiating. Are you guilty of giving away your ship? [FORMALLY SET YOUR PRICES IN WRITING such that you have decent high margins and then STICK TO THOSE PRICES NO MATTER WHAT. In any negotiation, you need to say up front that you retain the latitude to confer with your board and CPA and attorney before any agreement is finalized and signed.]

Non-performing and underperforming loans. Are you making full payment when partial payment or a smaller payment is or will be acceptable to your creditor? [Make arrangements to give partial payment for as long as possible. On the flip side, pay added principle as a way of eliminating interest.]

Offices. Are your gorgeous top management offices really necessary? [Is your huge gorgeous office building or edifice or suite really a deadly white heavy and burdensome cash eating albatross.]

OPM and Interest. Is there any sign your company is addicted to using other peoples' money? [Interest on other people's money never sleeps. At one point or another OPM will rise up and bite you and possibly eat you alive and this is true whether you use debt or equity OPM. You may be surprised, but equity OPM is often much more "SEC" and "litigation" and "loss of your business" dangerous than debt OPM.]

Opportunities. What are the ten most promising business opportunities that are readily apparent or hidden within your company?

Owner compensation. Are you pillaging your own company? [Should your first "turnaround" act be to cut your own compensation? You may think you are worth hundreds of thousands or millions of dollars but odds are you are not. How do your employees feel when you take down your hundreds of thousands or millions and they provide all the work and most of the brains and they take down their tens and hundreds? Excessive compensation is a recipe for an "off with their management heads" French Revolution.]

Performance data.*** Critical to any review of your business is performance data including but not limited to financial data:

1) profit and loss,
2) inventory,
3) profit margins,
4) cash flow,
5) accounts receivable,
6) investment performance,
7) debt repayment status.

Also to be considered are statistical indicators:

1) production units,
2) productive time,
3) work and projects-in-process,
4) time per project.

Performance data should be available for all segments of your business and in particularly from sales.

Persistence. Are you as persistent as you ought to be? [Persistence is tenaciously refusing to give up or quit.]

Notes:

Peter Drucker. His is one of the great business minds. Read his books if you have not already done so.

Planning. Stop everything you are doing for the next four hours and write your personal and business economic stimulus plan.

Policies and procedures. Are there policies and procedures that need to be written and implemented? [Can existing policies and procedures be simplified?]

Politics and infighting. Can you put a stop to destructive company politics and infighting? [Can you identify and squelch organizational politics and infighting? A turnaround is the time for what is best for the company not what is best for a particular individual or group or division.]

Power point and winging it. Are you in the habit of winging it in your presentations? [Prepare! And forget the power point unless absolutely necessary. Power point presentations waste time, energy and money. A short handout given out before, during or after the presentation is more effective.]

Prayer. Can you do everything by yourself or do you need the help of God? ["The object of prayer is not to change the will of God, but to secure for ourselves and for others blessings that God is already willing to grant, but that are made conditional on our asking for them." (Bible Dictionary, p. 753.) For what should we pray: "Cry unto him when ye are in your fields, yea, over all your flocks. Cry unto him in your houses, yea, over all your household, both morning, mid-day, and evening. Yea, cry unto him against the power of your enemies. Yea, cry unto him against the devil, who is an enemy to all righteousness. Cry unto him over the crops of your fields, that ye may prosper in them. Cry over the flocks of your fields, that they may increase. But this is not all; ye must pour out your souls in your closets, and your secret places, and in your wilderness. Yea, and when you do not cry unto the Lord, let your hearts be full, drawn out in prayer unto him continually for your welfare, and also for the welfare of those who are around you." (Book of Mormon, Alma 34:17-29]

Preparation and practice. Can you wing it and keep doing what you have been doing and have your business succeed? [Arguably not. Preparation and practice precede quality performance.]

Preventive accounting and finance. What preventive accounting and finance measures should be taken? [You may want to engage your CPA or accounting group in a preventive accounting and finance initiative.]

Preventive law. What preventive law steps can be taken to protect you and your business? [You may want to engage your attorney or attorneys in a preventive law initiative designed to identify those laws with which you must comply. Then take the initiative and comply.]

Printing. Are you using ink guzzling dinosaur printers? [Buy black and white and color printers and copiers that take little ink. Cheap printers can cost your company a small fortune because the cost of the ink is so high.]

Prices. Are you lowering or raising prices? [You may want to think seriously about raising all of your prices immediately. It may be that you cannot [and should not] lower your prices and still have adequate operating revenues unless you happen to be a Wal-Mart. The story is told of an owner of a turquoise jewelry shop in Arizona who was leaving on vacation. As she walked out the door of the shop she yelled back: "Mark everything down and sell it out by the time I get back!" The employee didn't listen or couldn't remember what she said and decided she must have said, "Mark everything up and sell it out by the time I get back." She dutifully marked everything up one hundred percent and ran a huge ad and sold everything out by the time the owner got back."]

Principles and values. Are you operating your business based on principles? [If you are not doing so already, write and focus your life and your business on a written set of core principles and values such as: excellence, quality, timeliness, speed to market, innovation, leadership, sensitivity, service, and work.]

Problems that are personal. What are the ten most serious problems you and your family are facing right now?

Problems that are work-related. Right now, what are the ten most serious problems you are facing that are work-related?

Procurement and buying. Do you have a trained procurement/buying officer and a computerized procurement/buying system? [Procurement/buying is an art form learned by hard study and experience. It involves documenting how you buy each item including details about suppliers and then it requires focus on how you can negotiate ethically and buy for less.]

Professional help. Do you need professional help to turn your business around? [Maybe so and maybe not. If so, own up to that fact and get yourself professional consulting and help from someone in your industry who has been there and done what you are trying to do.]

Profit margins that are eroding. Are your profit margins eroded or eroding? [Decreasing profit margins indicate your business is in trouble. Unless you can function at low prices like Wall-Mart, to compensate, try increasing your prices and cutting costs of manufacture and production.]

Profitability. Are you trying to run your business without being profitable? [The first cardinal rule of business is: ONLY THE PROFITABLE SURVIVE!]

Public speaking. Do you fear public speaking. [Prepare your remarks. Practice your remarks. Deliver your remarks. If you are prepared you will not fear.]

Notes:

Quality. Is your business selling poor quality goods and services? [Focus on quality as the best way to improve your bottom line. Quality products. Quality service. Quality sales. Quality relationships. Consider this summary of William Edwards Deming's 14 principles from his 1986 book *Out of the Crisis,* pages 23 and24.

1. "Create constancy of purpose toward improvement of product and service, with the aim to become competitive and stay in business, and to provide jobs. [Be resolute.]
2. "Adopt the new philosophy. We are in a new economic age. Western management must awaken to the challenge, must learn their responsibilities, and take on leadership for change. [The same old approach got you where you are. Only a new approach will get you where you want to be.]
3. "Cease dependence on inspection to achieve quality. Eliminate the need for inspection on a mass basis by building quality into the product in the first place. [Quality first not later.]
4. "End the practice of awarding business on the basis of price tag. Instead, minimize total cost. Move towards a single supplier for any one item, on a long-term relationship of loyalty and trust. [One risk however is becoming captive to one supplier and its fortunes.]
5. "Improve constantly and forever the system of production and service, to improve quality and productivity, and thus constantly decrease costs. [Forever better.]
6. "Institute training on the job. [On the job training and off the job training. Both are needed.]
7. "Institute leadership. The aim of supervision should be to help people and machines and gadgets to do a better job. Supervision of management is in need of overhaul, as well as supervision of production workers. [Your job is to provide the leadership.]
8. "Drive out fear, so that everyone may work effectively for the company. [Preparation is the antidote to fear.]
9. "Break down barriers between departments [and companies and universities and government organizations]. People in research, design, sales, and production must work as a team, to foresee problems of production and in use that may be encountered with the product or service. [The best ideas, processes, and products are not always invented here.]

10. "Eliminate slogans, exhortations, and targets for the work force asking for zero defects and new levels of productivity. Such exhortations only create adversarial relationships, as the bulk of the causes of low quality and low productivity belong to the system and thus lie beyond the power of the work force. [Focus on fixing and improving the system.]

11. a. "Eliminate work standards (quotas) on the factory floor. Substitute leadership. [It is probably do both.]
b. "Eliminate management by objective. Eliminate management by numbers, numerical goals. Substitute leadership. [Objectives, numbers, and numerical goals are important if workers have access to them. Couple these with leadership.]

12. a. "Remove barriers that rob the hourly worker of his right to pride of workmanship. The responsibility of supervisors must be changed from sheer numbers to quality. [Pride of ownership.]
b. "Remove barriers that rob people in management and in engineering of their right to pride of workmanship. This means, *inter alia,"* *abolishment of the annual or merit rating and of management by objective*. [My own take is we need a blend.]

13. "Institute a vigorous program of education and self-improvement. [Yes.]

14. "Put everybody in the company to work to accomplish the transformation. The transformation is everybody's job.

Training is needed to instill the courage to break with tradition.

(And see Wikipedia, W. Edwards Deming. For the detailed 14 Points see pages)

Quit. Are you tempted to throw in the towel and quit? [Don't! What is it Churchill said: Never, Never, Never give up!]

Relationships. Are you laboring under the assumption that all of your intra and inter company relationships are ok? [Make a list of your critical relationships including your business employees, colleagues, suppliers, professionals, other companies, and your bosses, spouse, children and grandchildren, and your neighbors, and focus on improving those relationships. Most relationships can be salvaged and improved by sharing a little bit more time and by listening.]

Reporting. After 4 HOURS of focused thought time, you should now have a written business economic stimulus plan that includes a checklist of issues and relationships and other matters that require fixing, change or implementation. It is important to involve your management and work teams in the process by letting them review your plan and make recommendations as to ways to implement what you have in mind. Your economic stimulus plan ought to be a working document without "pride of authorship." Its words should be set in soft putty not stone. Sending three or four drafts to management and worker teams for their comments is a valued way to obtain understanding, buy-in and implementation.

Research 1. What need is there for further product and market research? [Research is lifeblood to your product or service line.]

Research 2. Once you have written your economic stimulus plan and your list of issues and changes you want to address and implement, this is a good time for further research. Further discussions with management, workers, clients, customers, professional service providers, the public, focus groups, small groups, family, friends, neighbors, and competitors are in order. Other financial testing is in order. Talks with experts in the field are valuable. Discussions with your attorney and CPA and financial planner and insurance agent are valuable. Further research will provide evidence and confidence that you are on the right track, that the issues you are addressing are the most significant and critical. In this added research address criteria and standards. Look at conditions, causes, significance, and related recommendations. Work out more precise projections and detailed implementation costs as well as a pro forma.

Notes:

Revenue increase. One way to increase your revenues is by eliminating or minimizing the need to repeat the sale. [Consider subscriptions, royalties, affiliate and licensing opportunities. To the extent reasonable, get rid of revenue sources that require repeat sales. It usually costs you just as much time and money to set in place a sale that generates recurring revenues as it does to set in place a sale that generates "one time" revenue.]

Road or aisle or bridge. Are you willing to cross the road or aisle or bridge? [Most problems can be solved quickly and easily if you will just cross the road or aisle or bridge and listen to the person on the other side. Your empathy will go a long way toward creating understanding and consensus and positive action.

Sales 1. Sell! Sell! Sell! Bill! Bill! Bill! Collect! Collect! Collect! Nothing happens until something is sold, billed and collected! Again, nothing happens until something is sold, billed and collected! So there is good argument for getting out of your chair to sell face to face. Sell by telephone. Sell on television. Sell on the internet. Arguably, too many CEOs sit in their fortress office caves. The CEO and CIO and CFO and COO need to get out of the chairs and go out among the people and businesses and representatives and affiliates and suppliers and customers and sell their products and services and ideas and then bill and collect the money.

Notes:

Sales 2. Are those who sell your products and services selling without careful thinking and preparation? [Consider the concept of selling by the numbers. Sell and evaluate sales success by the number of calls. The number of appointments. The number of quality presentations. The number of closes. The number of signed contracts. The number of sales. The number of deliveries. The number billed. The number collected. The number resold.]

Sales decreasing. If your sales are falling, do something different. [Decreasing sales indicate trouble. Read "Who Moved My Cheese?"]

Sales/Selling by contract. Stop each and every oral sale or agreement or contract or deal immediately? [Tactfully or not so tactfully cut off such sales and focus only on sales that are memorialized in written agreements and contracts?]

Notes:

Sarbanes Oxley. If you are a public company, at some point you will have to stop avoiding hard study and get a grasp on Sarbanes Oxley regulations. [Ask your CPA and Attorney to brief and help you.]

Saving. Is there a way you can stop spending all revenues? [It is an old proverb that you should pay your business and yourself first by saving a minimum of ten percent of all you take in. I believe this is true and applies to the individual and the family and to small and large companies.]

Notes:

Security Systems. How good are your security systems? [Besides carrying insurance,

1) Do you have installed security systems in your buildings, plant, computers, software programs and files, physical files, in your car, in your home?
2) What kind of system do you use to guard your keys?
3) Your credit cards?
4) Your financial and other information?
5) Your computers?
6) Your software?
7) Your records?
8) The details about your family?
9) Your assets?
10) Your travel and daily movement itineraries?
11) Do you know who you are dealing with before you grant them access to your shop or plant or clean room or warehouse or storage unit or office or home or product line?
12) Have you trained your employees in what to do when there is a breach of security?
13) There is a lot of common sense in good security.
14) There is also a realm of high tech professional security that is far beyond simple security systems and plans.
15) If you make a great deal of money you may need a professional company to set up your security systems and safe rooms and safe places.
16) You may need a body guard to protect your body and the persons of your spouse and kids and key employees.
17) In all security situations, pay attention.
18) If it feels funny it is funny.
19) Pay attention to intuitive thoughts when they hit you.
20) Thoughts that stand your hair up on the back of your neck.
21) Thoughts that make you feel something is just not right.]
22) And do you have backup copies of your documents and media pictures, audio, and video.

Notes:

Sensitivity. Are you or other management or professional persons running rough shod over your support staff and line officers? [You shouldn't allow this to happen. If you are not sensitive, you will find that you have little support including social, emotional and physical protection from those with whom you work. Your staff and your line will sabotage your efforts as payback for any lack of sensitivity and any display of egotism.]

Sexual and physical harassment, bullying and bigotry. Is there sexual or physical harassment, bullying, or bigotry by yourself or among your employees or co-workers or management? [Periodically, call your people together and review your policies and tell your people to leave if they can't leave one another alone verbally and physically. Sexual and bigoted comments, jokes, innuendo, advances and bullying threats destroy workplace morale and relationships.]

Shareholders and directors and your boss. Are you or your people ignoring your shareholders and your board of directors and your Bosses? [Set up a system to communicate with them on a consistent basis. Communicate with your largest shareholders and with your board of directors and your bosses personally and not through memos and other people.]

Notes:

To buy a hard copy of one of my books, click on www.amazon.com and click on books and type in the title or my name.

Simplify. Are there ways you can cut the complexity and simplify? [You can simplify most any procedure or process if you set your mind to it. With very little effort, you and your business can be much more user friendly. You can simplify immediately and deliver faster and better products and services to your customers if you put your mind to it.]

Software and physical records. Are you trying to run your business out of your brain without the aid of software or physical records? [Inevitably you will forget and make a mistake. As a corollary, to the extent you can, run your business as a virtual business via software and the internet. Use software and a physical calendar so you have redundant calendars and don't forget meetings and deadlines. And in all this, don't forget to back up your information and records and computer software and systems.]

Statistics. Are you monitoring progress with weekly statistics and financial numbers? [It goes without saying that numbers are the primary language of any business. Keep track and BEAT YESTERDAY'S PERFORMANCE!]

Notes:

Stinginess. Are you stingy with your money and your products and services? [See the paragraph above on giving.]

Stock. Are you tight with your stock? [Incent your people by giving them significant blocks of pre-trading or trading stock.]

Stock and going public if yours is a small company. If yours is a small company with little or no revenues, stop worrying about and spending your time trying to go public by reverse merger or pink sheet or over the counter. [The best use of your time until your company is generating significant monthly revenues is to spend your time making sales.]

Stop to consider if you are acting like the Emperor. Are you or any of your management team operating your business like that of the emperor "Alittle Kingly" who was conned into walking around without his clothes? [Unless the emperor is engaged in turning around and improving his or her kingdom, a person on the parade route or in the stadium including perhaps a journalist is likely to laugh and shout: "The emperor does not have on any clothes!" So give some serious thought to the wisdom of stopping your relationship with anyone or anything that is conning you into walking around without your clothes. Stop means stop doing what you have always done in the past. Forget your golf games and racket ball and parties and entertaining and lunches and hot cars and big houses and perks and benefits and focus on writing your personal and business A-Z economic stimulus plan. Stop and turn your company around. "Without clothes" means nakedly working without benefit of written principles and plans and initiatives and sales and billings and collections and money needed to stay in business and grow the business. "Without clothes" means walking around naked because you have been lulled into a false sense of security that it could never happen to you or conned into some strange scheme by one or more of your less than full wattage managers or employees or family or acquaintances.

Notes:

Success. Are you focusing your life on money and SUCCESS. [Success is a byproduct of doing right things and doing things right means doing things according to a set of right and high principles. Success is a byproduct of helping others get what they want. Success is also a result of avoiding failure events.]

Suppliers. Are your people guilty of changing suppliers just for a price break? [Consider Deming's advice about getting one or a couple of good suppliers and staying loyal.]

Supply. How limited is your supply of materials? [Are you prepared for emergencies? Do you have a supply of production materials on hand in case there is a shortage?]

Survey 1. How certain are you that you know what people really think? [You may want to conduct a series of informal and formal and even "anonymous" surveys to obtain correct information about how you and your company are perceived. How you and your company are viewed has bearing on what changes you need to and can make to be or remain profitable.]

Notes:

Survey stage of your internal and operational audit.*** The survey stage of an internal or operational audit is used to find out what is going on within your organization. The purpose of this audit stage is to understand and write up as accurately as possible in carefully written and indexed audit papers what is actually happening within your financial, legal, management, and operational systems. Such audit analysis takes into account

1) the outside environment including the state of the economy, competition, laws, regulations, technology, political climate, outside and even foreign relationships and regulations, demographics, and maturity of the business.

2) It documents the company environment including interfacing organizations, company plans and strategies, company policy, products and services and pricing.

3) It reviews company objectives and plans including shifts in manufacturing or marketing or sales strategy, rates of growth, changes in products and services, formality and communication of plans.

4) It documents company policy and key procedures including compensation, conflict of interest, non-competes, pricing, purchasing, and other vital procedures for key company activities.

5) It looks at the organization complication and decentralization and flow of work and spans of control and role definitions and line, staff, and support personnel.

6) It considers personnel skill levels, management styles, loyalty, morale, age, relationship, legal compliance, drug free and harassment policies.

7) It looks at the physical location of plant and offices and warehousing and distances to key markets and age of plant and equipment and deferred maintenance as well as use of plant and equipment and available technology as well as capital structure.

8) It looks at systems and data flows including flow of information to management, reports, inputs, documentation, sophistication of computer and other information equipment and applications and software and systems.

9) It looks at the internal controls over finances and other assets and authorization procedures, the accuracy of financial and other information and compliance reporting.

10) It takes a critical look at your compliance with standards of performance and with laws and regulations.

Taxes. Are you paying federal and state and payroll and sales taxes blindly? [Ask your CPA to give you a list of the ways you can save federal and state and payroll and sales taxes legitimately and implement his or her suggestions. Set aside time and resources for competent professional tax planning.]

Taxes, delay in filing and paying. Are any of your accounting people or others delaying payment of your taxes, and especially payroll and FICA taxes? [You may want to keep in mind the fact that you are personally liable if you let your tax obligation get out of control and go unfiled and unpaid and that a criminal conviction comes with stiff penalties including fines and jail time and a civil determination also carries stiff repayment fines.]

Notes:

To buy a hard copy of one of my books, click on www.amazon.com and click on books and type in the title or my name.

Team of advisors. Who are two or three trusted advisors who will tell you the truth? [Ask your trusted advisors for help -- your CPA, attorney, banker, partner, (wife or husband or son or daughter or brother or sister university professor or other relative, etc.)]

Technology. Are you operating in the dark ages without benefit of technology? [If you should be more aggressive at using technology, buy it or develop it.]

Telephones. Are your telephone expenses out of control? Are your telephones being answered properly? [You may want to task one of your people to work with cell and regular phone and internet providers to cut your telephone expense. Have someone call your telephones and dollars to donuts you will find that many of your employees do not answer their telephones. And this is especially true of banks.]

Ten per day? If sales do not come to you automatically, you may want to think about doing the following. [Notwithstanding all of "THE SECRET" "LAW OF ATTRACTION" hype which says change your thoughts and things will automatically come to you, unless you and your sales persons make at least five or ten calls per day, you won't fill your pipeline and as a consequence you won't close the sales you need to stay alive and grow. "No sales" equates to no revenue! "No revenue" equates to no profit! "No profit" equates to no business! No amount of positive "Law of Attraction" thinking without action will produce sales. You can't sell your product to a desk in your office. So again, you may want to get on the phone and get out of the office and meet face to face with your potential clients. Be the sales catalyst for the company in prospecting, presenting, and closing sales.]

Notes:

Theft. What is your mindset about your employees and others and whether they will or won't steal from you? [You may want to meet with your employees periodically and tell them you expect and trust them to be honest. Notwithstanding, you need to be careful. You need to guard your flank. It is vital that you have controls like time clocks, inventory tracking, equipment check out and check in systems, accounting, purchasing and travel controls, and auditing systems, each designed in part to protect your company from theft, embezzlement and fraud.]

Things not to do list. Do you carry a things to do list or a things not to do list or both? [Most managers and knowledge workers have been raised on mission, goals, objectives, and things to do lists – on management by objective theories and systems. You should also carry a "things not to do" list and at the same time you should mandate that all employees develop and carry a "things not to do" list as part of their mission, goals, objectives, and things to do lists and plans.]

Tools. Are you wasting your tools? [Tools left out in the rain rust. Tools left out in the open are stolen. Tools not serviced become useless. Tools not inventoried and put away get lost or stolen.]

Training. What training programs are or ought to be provided? [Mandate that each employee read and study and train for the job. Professional people like attorneys and CPAs are required to complete so many hours of continuing education each year including a certain number of ethics related training hours. Regardless of how training is provided, each person needs make the personal effort to be competent at his or her job or find another job elsewhere.]

Travel. Is any travel taken without your pre-determined approval? Do you have a policy in place that prohibits all travel expense except for sales trips you sign off on personally and in advance. [As a way of cutting travel expense, you may want to encourage your sales people to make distant sales via company phone, cell phone, conference call, email, video phone, or video conference.]

Notes:

55

Truth. Is there any lying going on in your organization about products and services and success or failure. [Do you have a written policy mandating silence on certain matters and at the same time requiring telling the truth to colleagues, partners, bankers, attorneys, suppliers, CPAs, stock brokers, IRS, SEC, and other financial and sales persons.]

Venture capitalists and venture capital. Is there a way you can avoid using Venture Capitalists and Venture Capital? [Venture Capitalists can eat up more than half your company. Rather than focusing your energies on obtaining venture capital, focus your energies on quality sales. And again, keep in mind when you think in terms of the risks of using OPM, venture capital is usually far more onerous than debt capital.]

Video, TV & Radio, and Internet. Contrary to the thought that you can put everything on one page, you may have to stop doing all of your communicating by written memo or email. [You may need to create a video or audio presentation or go on TV or radio or Internet Facebook or other social networking system, or the intracompany information system to explain a particular matter or situation. If you find that you need to do so, you may be better off hiring a professional PR person to help you.]

Virtual company. Is there really a need to expand your infrastructure and build more buildings? [Is there a way to build a virtual company instead? Keep in mind that this is the age when one person in India can own and operate a world-wide multi-million dollar business and compete globally from a few internet driven computer terminals in Bangalore.]

Wealth recovery and retention. Is there really a way you can recover lost wealth or retain the wealth you generate using the same old strategies and tactics? [Times have changed. Technology has transformed the world. Old systems are slow if not obsolete. To recover lost wealth, to retain the wealth you have generated, you probably have to embrace technology and radically change the way you do business.]

Notes:

Will and trust and tax planning. Do you have a will and a trust? [Set aside time for professional estate and tax planning.]

Work ethic. Is there a flagging work ethic in your company? [You can set the example by being at the office early, by getting your project work done ahead of schedule, by performing your work noticeably well. You can leave late. Yet you ought to take your holidays and vacation.]

Writing and speaking and verbosity. Are you or your management team verbose? [You may need to work at cutting to the chase, at writing your memos one page front only -- one paragraph may be better -- one sentence may be better. In this age, less tends to be more valued than more.]

You're fired! You may want to stop what you are doing and fire those who are not part of your solution. [Again, it is what a person does not what a person says that determines if he or she goes or stays.]

You're hired! You may want to stop what you are doing and identify and retain or hire the right person. [He or she may already be working in your organization. Maybe it is your spouse? Maybe one of your children? Maybe a trusted friend? Maybe someone who has learned the business from the ground up.]

Sources:

1. **My own experience and writing over a number of years.**
2. **References listed throughout the document.**
3. **Wikipedia. Internet.**
4. **Internet.**
5. ***** Personal audit checklists and papers from the time I worked as an internal auditor.**

"Alittle Kingly" © 2009.

To buy a hard copy of one of my books, click on <u>www.amazon.com</u> and click on books and type in the title or my name.

Worksheets. Use these or develop your own spreadsheets. Then sit at your computer and write your own economic stimulus plan.

Sales Product or Service	Cost of Goods Cost of Service	Annual Unit Sales	Annual $ Sales	Monthly Unit Sales	Monthly $ Sales	Sales Commissions	Net to Business

Sales Product or Service	Cost of Goods Cost of Service	Annual Unit Sales	Annual $ Sales	Monthly Unit Sales	Monthly $ Sales	Sales Commissions	Net to Business

Sales Product or Service	Cost of Goods Cost of Service	Annual Unit Sales	Annual $ Sales	Monthly Unit Sales	Monthly $ Sales	Sales Commissions	Net to Business

62

Sales Product or Service	Cost of Good Cost of Service	Annual Unit Sales	Annual $ Sales	Monthly Unit Sales	Monthly $ Sales	Sales Commissions	Net to Business

	Collections	Amount	When	Who is	Status			
	Accounts	Due	Due	Responsible				

64

Collections Accounts	Amount Due	When Due	Who is Responsible	Status			

Collections Accounts	Amount Due	When Due	Who is Responsible	Status			

Collections **Accounts**	**Amount** **Due**	**When** **Due**	**Who is** **Responsible**	**Status**			

Debts Creditors	Original Amt Of Debt	Payment Amount	Payment Due Date	Amount Owning	Payments Remaining	Interest Rate	Status

Debts Creditors	Original Amt Of Debt	Payment Amount	Payment Due Date	Amount Owning	Payments Remaining	Interest Rate	Status

Debts Creditors	Original Amt Of Debt	Payment Amount	Payment Due Date	Amount Owning	Payments Remaining	Interest Rate	Status

Debts Creditors	Original Amt Of Debt	Payment Amount	Payment Due Date	Amount Owning	Payments Remaining	Interest Rate	Status

Expenses		Expenses		Expenses		Expenses	
Advertising		Insurance Life		Taxes Income		Other	
Airplane(s)		Internet Service		Taxes Payroll			
Automobile(s)		Lease 1		Taxes Property			
Cell Phones & Service		Lease 2		Taxes Sales			
Clothing		Legal Services		Telephone			
Consulting		Maintenance		Television			
Debt Service		Marketing		Tools			
Debt Mortgage 1		Payroll		Transportation			
Debt Mortgage 2		Printing		Travel			
Diesel		Professional Services		Web Develop.			
Domains		Propane					
Electricity		Public Relations					
Equipment		Rent					
Gasoline		Repairs					
Heating		Retirement					
Hosting Web		Sales Commissions					
Insurance		Security					
Insurance Casualty		Supplies for Office					
Insurance Earthquake		Supplies Products					
Insurance Errors & O.							
Insurance Key Man							

Expenses		Expenses		Expenses		Expenses	
Advertising		Insurance Life		Taxes Income		Other	
Airplane(s)		Internet Service		Taxes Payroll			
Automobile(s)		Lease 1		Taxes Property			
Cell Phones & Service		Lease 2		Taxes Sales			
Clothing		Legal Services		Telephone			
Consulting		Maintenance		Television			
Debt Service		Marketing		Tools			
Debt Mortgage 1		Payroll		Transportation			
Debt Mortgage 2		Printing		Travel			
Diesel		Professional Services		Web Develop.			
Domains		Propane					
Electricity		Public Relations					
Equipment		Rent					
Gasoline		Repairs					
Heating		Retirement					
Hosting Web		Sales Commissions					
Insurance		Security					
Insurance Casualty		Supplies for Office					
Insurance Earthquake		Supplies Products					
Insurance Errors & O.							
Insurance Key Man							

Expenses		Expenses		Expenses		Expenses	
Advertising		Insurance Life		Taxes Income		Other	
Airplane(s)		Internet Service		Taxes Payroll			
Automobile(s)		Lease 1		Taxes Property			
Cell Phones & Service		Lease 2		Taxes Sales			
Clothing		Legal Services		Telephone			
Consulting		Maintenance		Television			
Debt Service		Marketing		Tools			
Debt Mortgage 1		Payroll		Transportation			
Debt Mortgage 2		Printing		Travel			
Diesel		Professional Services		Web Develop.			
Domains		Propane					
Electricity		Public Relations					
Equipment		Rent					
Gasoline		Repairs					
Heating		Retirement					
Hosting Web		Sales Commissions					
Insurance		Security					
Insurance Casualty		Supplies for Office					
Insurance Earthquake		Supplies Products					
Insurance Errors & O.							
Insurance Key Man							

Expenses		Expenses		Expenses		Expenses	
Advertising		Insurance Life		Taxes Income		Other	
Airplane(s)		Internet Service		Taxes Payroll			
Automobile(s)		Lease 1		Taxes Property			
Cell Phones & Service		Lease 2		Taxes Sales			
Clothing		Legal Services		Telephone			
Consulting		Maintenance		Television			
Debt Service		Marketing		Tools			
Debt Mortgage 1		Payroll		Transportation			
Debt Mortgage 2		Printing		Travel			
Diesel		Professional Services		Web Develop.			
Domains		Propane					
Electricity		Public Relations					
Equipment		Rent					
Gasoline		Repairs					
Heating		Retirement					
Hosting Web		Sales Commissions					
Insurance		Security					
Insurance Casualty		Supplies for Office					
Insurance Earthquake		Supplies Products					
Insurance Errors & O.							
Insurance Key Man							

Payroll Personnel by Name	Monthly	Annual	Payroll Tax	Retirement	Other Benefits	Notes	

Payroll							
Personnel by Name	Monthly	Annual	Payroll Tax	Retirement	Other Benefits	Notes	

Payroll							
Personnel by Name	Monthly	Annual	Payroll Tax	Retirement	Other Benefits	Notes	

Payroll							
Personnel by Name	Monthly	Annual	Payroll Tax	Retirement	Other Benefits	Notes	

Turnaround Checklist	Action Steps						
1							
2							
3							
4							
5							
6							
7							
8							
9							
10							
11							
12							
13							
14							
15							
16							
17							
18							
19							
20							

Turnaround Checklist	Action Steps						
1							
2							
3							
4							
5							
6							
7							
8							
9							
10							
11							
12							
13							
14							
15							
16							
17							
18							
19							
20							

Turnaround Checklist	Action Steps						
1							
2							
3							
4							
5							
6							
7							
8							
9							
10							
11							
12							
13							
14							
15							
16							
17							
18							
19							
20							

Turnaround Checklist	Action Steps					
1						
2						
3						
4						
5						
6						
7						
8						
9						
10						
11						
12						
13						
14						
15						
16						
17						
18						
19						
20						

Turnaround Checklist	Action Steps						
1							
2							
3							
4							
5							
6							
7							
8							
9							
10							
11							
12							
13							
14							
15							
16							
17							
18							
19							
20							

Turnaround Checklist	Action Steps						
1							
2							
3							
4							
5							
6							
7							
8							
9							
10							
11							
12							
13							
14							
15							
16							
17							
18							
19							
20							

Turnaround Checklist	Action Steps						
1							
2							
3							
4							
5							
6							
7							
8							
9							
10							
11							
12							
13							
14							
15							
16							
17							
18							
19							
20							

Turnaround Checklist	Action Steps						
1							
2							
3							
4							
5							
6							
7							
8							
9							
10							
11							
12							
13							
14							
15							
16							
17							
18							
19							
20							

Turnaround Checklist	Action Steps					
1						
2						
3						
4						
5						
6						
7						
8						
9						
10						
11						
12						
13						
14						
15						
16						
17						
18						
19						
20						

Turnaround Checklist	Action Steps						
1							
2							
3							
4							
5							
6							
7							
8							
9							
10							
11							
12							
13							
14							
15							
16							
17							
18							
19							
20							

Footnote: Dr. W. Edwards Deming's 14 Points

1. **Constancy of purpose.** Create constancy of purpose for continual improvement of products and service to society, allocating resources to provide for long range needs rather than only short term profitability, with a plan to become competitive, to stay in business and to provide jobs.

2. **The new philosophy.** Adopt the new philosophy. We are in a new economic age, created in Japan. We can no longer live with commonly accepted levels of delays, mistakes, defective materials, and defective workmanship. Transformation of Western management style is necessary to halt the continued decline of business and industry.

3. **Cease dependence on mass inspection.** Eliminate the need for mass inspection as the way of life to achieve quality by building quality into the product in the first place. Require statistical evidence of built in quality in both manufacturing and purchasing functions.

4. **End lowest tender contracts.** End the practice of awarding business solely on the basis of price tag. Instead require meaningful measures of quality along with price. Reduce the number of suppliers for the same item by eliminating those that do not qualify with statistical and other evidence of quality. The aim is to minimize total cost, not merely initial cost, by minimizing variation. This may be achieved by moving toward a single supplier for any one item, on a long term relationship of loyalty and trust. Purchasing managers have a new job, and must learn it.

5. **Improve every process.** Improve constantly and forever every process for planning, production, and service. Search continually for problems in order to improve every activity in the company, to improve quality and productivity, and thus to constantly decrease costs. Institute innovation and constant improvement of product, service, and process. It is management's job to work continually on the system (design, incoming materials, maintenance, improvement of machines, supervision, training, retraining).

6. **Institute training on the job.** Institute modern methods of training on the job for all, including management, to make better use of every employee. New skills are required to keep up with changes in materials, methods, product and service design, machinery, techniques, and service.

7. **Institute leadership.** Adopt and institute leadership aimed at helping people do a better job. The responsibility of managers and supervisors must be changed from sheer numbers to quality. Improvement of quality will automatically improve productivity. Management must ensure that immediate action is taken on reports of inherited defects, maintenance requirements, poor tools, fuzzy operational definitions, and all conditions detrimental to quality.

8. **Drive out fear.** Encourage effective two way communication and other means to drive out fear throughout the organization so that everybody may work effectively and more productively for the company.

9. **Break down barriers.** Break down barriers between departments and staff areas. People in different areas, such as Leasing, Maintenance, Administration, must work in teams to tackle problems that may be encountered with products or service.

10. **Eliminate exhortations.** Eliminate the use of slogans, posters and exhortations for the work force, demanding Zero Defects and new levels of productivity, without providing methods. Such exhortations only create adversarial relationships; the bulk of the causes of low quality and low productivity belong to the system, and thus lie beyond the power of the work force.

11. **Eliminate arbitrary numerical targets.** Eliminate work standards that prescribe quotas for the work force and numerical goals for people in management. Substitute aids and helpful leadership in order to achieve continual improvement of quality and productivity.

12. **Permit pride of workmanship.** Remove the barriers that rob hourly workers, and people in management, of their right to pride of workmanship. This implies, among other things, abolition of the annual merit rating (appraisal of performance) and of Management by Objective. Again, the responsibility of managers, supervisors, foremen must be changed from sheer numbers to quality.

13. **Encourage education.** Institute a vigorous program of education, and encourage self improvement for everyone. What an organization needs is not just good people; it needs people that are improving with education. Advances in competitive position will have their roots in knowledge.

14. **Top management commitment and action.** Clearly define top management's permanent commitment to ever improving quality and productivity, and their obligation to implement all of these principles. Indeed, it is not enough that top management commit themselves for life to quality and productivity. They must know what it is that they are committed to – that is, what they must do. Create a structure in top management that will push every day on the preceding 13 Points, and take action in order to accomplish the transformation. Support is not enough: action is required!

15. **(Source: Out of The Crisis, W. Edwards Deming; Leadership Institute, Inc., http://www.lii.net/deming.html)**

We will be judged for the good or evil we think, say and do.

Story. Andrew Chipman's Christmas Angel, p. 4.

Some interesting footnotes, p. 43.

See author's blog at http://jesus-isthechrist.blogspot.com/

Order the author's books at www.amazon.com.

Andrew Chipman's Christmas Angel

Richard W. Linford

Barcode Area
We will add the barcode for you.
Made with Cover Creator

"Jesus Christ is King of Kings, Lord of Lords, and Savior of the World. He will soon return to usher in His great Millennial reign of peace, prosperity and love!" Richard Linford

* "Would Jesus Christ Do That? is the first question!" "What Would Jesus Do?" is the second question! -- a fiction short story.

* The New Testament Gospel of John with the words of Jesus Christ in bold -- non-fiction.

* Several author's notes you may find of great interest and perhaps even invaluable.

The author is a Christian -- a member of The Church of Jesus Christ of Latter-day Saints (the Mormons), family man, a bishop, attorney at law, businessman, and former state chairman and national board member of The NCCJ -- National Conference of Christians, Jews [and Muslims], a writer, artist and sometime golfer.

Barcode Area

We will add the barcode for you.

Made with Cover Creator

Would Jesus Christ Do That? is the first question!

What Would Jesus Do? is the second question!

Richard W Linford

"The Young Marine and the Snow" allegory is a story of Andrew Chipman's experience in the snows of the Bookcliff Mountains.

It is an allegory, symbolic of spiritual meanings and truths by means of concrete, visceral illustrations.

The story is of Andrew's life and death experiences including confrontation with great cougars -- evil and good, wrong and right, darkness and light, temptation and integrity, death and life. My allegory is a story of courage, survival and triumph.

To your great health, happiness, and prosperity!

Richard Linford

Barcode Area
We will add the barcode for you
Made with Cover Creator

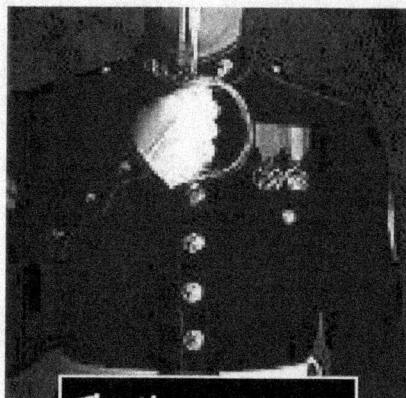

The Young Marine and the Snow
an allegory

Richard W. Linford

199 Ways To Make Your Good Marriage Great or Your Bad Marriage Better

ROMANCE AND IMPROVE YOUR MARRIAGE TODAY

RICHARD W. LINFORD

21. COMPLIMENTING ... BECAUSE HONEST, FAIR, KIND COMPLIMENTS EVERY DAY ARE ENDEARING ... BECAUSE WORDS OF APPROVAL ARE WORDS OF LOVE ... BECAUSE YOU CAN COMPLIMENT YOUR SPOUSE VERBALLY OR, BY EMAIL OR BY CARD ... BECAUSE BY COMPLIMENTING YOUR SPOUSE YOU HELP LIFT HER OR HIM TO HIGHER, BETTER, MORE CAPABLE LEVELS ... BECAUSE THE WORLD IS HARSH AND YOUR APPROVAL AND COMPLIMENTS MINIMIZE FEAR, FRUSTRATION AND ANXIETY.

22. CONCERTS ... BECAUSE THE SYMPHONY, A ROCK AND ROLL BAND, A YOUTUBE DATE TO WATCH FAVORITES PROVIDES COMMON, MEMORABLE MUSICAL EXPERIENCES THAT BIND YOU TOGETHER.

23. CONFIDENCE ... BECAUSE MOST EVERYTHING CAN WORK OUT ALL RIGHT IF YOU TRUST, BE WORTHY OF THE CONFIDENCE PLACED IN YOU BY YOUR SPOUSE.

24. CONTRIBUTING TO YOUR SPOUSE'S EMOTIONAL BANK ACCOUNT ... BECAUSE DAILY DEPOSITS TO YOUR SPOUSE'S EMOTIONAL WELL-BEING HELP BUILD BALANCES SUFFICIENT TO SUPPORT WITHDRAWALS.

25. CONTROLLING HOW YOU ARGUE ... BECAUSE SETTING GROUND RULES ABOUT HOW YOU ARGUE, HELPS TO ENSURE THAT YOUR ARGUMENTS WILL NOT BE CRITICAL, DIVISIVE, OR HURTFUL ... BECAUSE EACH PERSON SHOULD HAVE OPPORTUNITY TO STATE HIS POINT OF VIEW IN A PEACEFUL, CALM SETTING ... BECAUSE REASONING TOGETHER IS SO MUCH BETTER THAN ARGUING.

Barcode Area
We will add the barcode for you.
Made with Cover Creator

To buy a hard copy of one of my books,
click on www.amazon.com and click on books
and type in the title of the book or my name Richard W. Linford.

My business turnaround blog is
http://ceostrategies.blogspot.com/

STOP STROLLING AROUND NAKED IN YOUR BUSINESS EMPIRE LIKE "ALITTLE KINGLY"

"ALITTLE KINGLY"
™ © COPYRIGHT 2009

Put on some business turnaround threads
in the next 24 HOURS!

Write your own A-Z Economic Stimulus Plan
Improve quality
Ramp sales
Reduce expenses
Take advantage of a battered economy
Jump start your business
Supercharge yourself and your employees
Turn your business around
and
Stop being "Alittle Kingly"

Richard W. Linford